Raving Rum

Recipes

Make Delicious Rum Recipes for Any
Occasion

By

Heston Brown

HESTON BROWN

Copyright 2019 Heston Brown

Table of Contents

Introduction 6

Lime Daiquiri 7

Mojito 9

Hurricane Cocktail 11

Classic Pina Colada 13

Hot Buttered Rum 15

Rum Punch 17

Dark and Stormy 19

Captain Morgan Rum Sour 21

Wiki Wiki Cocktail 23

Peach Rum Cocktail 25

Paranubes Raspberry Cocktail 27

Caribbean Coco 29

Pineapple Love 31

Tropical Bliss 33

Tortuga Rum Blend.. 35

Rum Babalu 37

Rum Fruit Punch.. 39

Pina Colada 41

Strawberry Pineapple Cocktail........................... 43

Monkey Business.. 45

Blue Rum.. 47

Goldeneye Pineapple.. 49

Wild Cherry 51

Caribbean Queen 53

Boozy Gelato.. 55

Pineapple Ginger Cocktail................................. 57

Old Fashioned Bacardi 59

Mai Tai 61

The Huntmans 63

Island Mule 65

Conclusion.. 67

About the Author.. 68

Author's Afterthoughts.. 70

Introduction

Whether it's a Caribbean Coco made with delicious coconut rum and coconut yogurt or a simple, yet delicious Pineapple Express, these recipes are sure to please. This book is packed with tropical fruit drinks, creamy rum cocktails and more… all of which are absolutely amazing.

Grab the mint leaves or lime wedges for garnish and let's get partying! These recipes are made to serve two people but can always be doubled or even tripled for more people.

Lime Daiquiri

This daiquiri is super easy to make. All you need is rum, lime juice and simple syrup. Toss in some fresh lime wedges and cherries and enjoy!

Servings: 2

Prep Time: 5 minutes

Ingredients:

- 4 ounces of lime juice
- 2 ounce simple syrup
- 2 ounces Castillo white rum

Instructions:

1. Shake mixture with ice and strain into a martini glass.

2. Garnish with lime wedges and cherries.

Mojito

This is also another super easy drink to make. The lime and mint flavours come together quite nicely and makes this drink very refreshing.

Servings: 2

Prep Time: 5 minutes

Ingredients:

- 1 ounce of lime juice
- 1 ounce simple syrup
- 2 ounces Wray & Nephew white rum
- 4 ounces citrus soda
- ¼ cup crushed mint leaves

Instructions:

1. Shake mixture with ice and strain into a jar.

2. Garnish with lime wedges and mint leaves.

Hurricane Cocktail

This fruity cocktail includes both light and dark rum and delicious orange and passion fruit juice. The flavour profiles make it so delicious. Garnish with orange slices and cherries.

Servings: 2

Prep Time: 5 minutes

Ingredients:

- 0.5 ounce of lime juice
- 0.5 ounce grenadine
- 1 ounce simple syrup
- 1 ounce Wray & Nephew white rum
- 1 ounce Appleton Estate dark rum
- 2 ounces orange juice
- 2 ounces passion fruit juice

Instructions:

1. Shake mixture with ice and strain into a glass.

Classic Pina Colada

This signature Caribbean drink is famous for a reason. Coconut and pineapple are simply amazing together, mix in some white rum and garnish with cherries.

Servings: 2

Prep Time: 5 minutes

Ingredients:

- 2 ounces Mount Gay Premium white rum
- 3 ounces pineapple juice
- 3 ounces coconut cream

Instructions:

1. Blend ingredients with ice or shake mixture with ice and strain into a glass.

Hot Buttered Rum

This warm rum will definitely hit the spot on a cold day or night. The rum itself warms the body and so does this sweet, spicy warm drink.

Servings: 1

Prep Time: 5 minutes

Ingredients:

- 2 ounces Appleton Special Gold rum
- 1 teaspoon vanilla extract
- 1 teaspoon brown sugar
- 1 teaspoon melted butter
- 1 teaspoon cinnamon

Instructions:

1. Shake ingredients except butter over ice.

2. Pour in melted butter.

Rum Punch

This rum punch is super refreshing. It's a great blend of different fruit juices and dark rum. Garnish with cherries and orange slices.

Servings: 2

Prep Time: 5 minutes

Ingredients:

- 3 ounces Appleton Special Gold rum
- 2 ounces pineapple juice
- 2 ounces passion fruit juice
- 1 ounce cherry juice

Instructions:

1. Pour rum into glasses filled with ice.

2. Pour in pineapple, passion fruit and cherry juice.

Dark and Stormy

This drink will help you get over a dark and stormy day. The flavour of the classic black seal rum used and ginger beer is divine for a rum lover.

Servings: 2

Prep Time: 5 minutes

Ingredients:

- 2 ounces Gosling's Black Seal rum
- 2 ounces ginger beer

Instructions:

1. Pour ingredients into glasses with ice.

Captain Morgan Rum Sour

This popular recipe calls for a delicious flavour combination of Captain Morgan rum, fresh lemon sour and simple syrup.

Servings: 2

Prep Time: 5 minutes

Ingredients:

- 2 ounces Captain Morgan rum
- 2 ounces fresh lemon sour
- 2 ounces simple syrup

Instructions:

1. Pour ingredients into glasses with ice.

Wiki Wiki Cocktail

Having and making this drink is just as fun as saying its name. This sweet drink is refreshing and a sure pleasure to your taste buds.

Servings: 2

Prep Time: 5 minutes

Ingredients:

- 3 ounces Blanc Rhum Agricole
- 0.5 ounce mango brandy
- 0.5 ounce mango Mount Gay rum
- 2 ounces lime juice
- 2 ounces pineapple juice
- 1 ounce cane syrup
- 1 kiwi, peeled

Instructions:

1. Muddle kiwi in tall glasses.

2. Pour other ingredients into glasses and add crushed ice.

Peach Rum Cocktail

The slightly tart flavour of the lime juice in this cocktail is accompanied by gold rum and peach rum! Yum!

Servings: 2

Prep Time: 5 minutes

Ingredients:

- 2 ounces Appleton Special Gold rum
- 2 ounces Bacardi Peach rum
- 1 ounce lime juice
- 3 ounces orange juice

Instructions:

1. Shake ingredients over ice.

2. Pour into glasses.

Paranubes Raspberry Cocktail

This tart and sweet cocktail is simply delicious. Just a few ingredients, a little shake and you're good to go! Garnish with fresh raspberries and lime wedges.

Servings: 2

Prep Time: 5 minutes

Ingredients:

- 3 ounces Paranubes rum
- 1 ounce lime juice
- 1 ounce raspberry juice
- 0.5 ounce simple syrup
- 3.5 ounces club soda

Instructions:

1. Shake ingredients over ice.

Caribbean Coco

Make this for your next get together and everyone will be amazed! Delicious coconut flavoured rum paired with coconut yogurt and of course… rum! Serve in a coconut to give it more of a Caribbean feel and garnish with mint.

Servings: 2

Prep Time: 5 minutes

Ingredients:

- 2 ounces El Dorado rum
- 2 ounces Clement Coco rhum
- 1 teaspoon coconut milk yogurt
- 1 ounce simple syrup
- 1 ounce lime juice
- Mint for garnish

Instructions:

1. Shake ingredients over ice and garnish with mint.

Pineapple Love

This is for all the pineapple lovers out there. Pineapple rum plus pineapple syrup and a dash of lime juice, there's really nothing more you can ask for.

Servings: 2

Prep Time: 5 minutes

Ingredients:

- 4 ounces Pineapple rum blend
- 1 ounce lime juice
- 1 ounce pineapple syrup

Instructions:

1. Stir ingredients together.

Tropical Bliss

This drink combines delicious fruit flavours, lime juice and honey. Garnish with mint and tropical edible flowers. Top with a pinch of salt in each.

Servings: 2

Prep Time: 5 minutes

Ingredients:

- 3 ounces Appleton Special rum
- 0.5 ounce spiced pineapple syrup
- 1 ounce honey syrup
- 1 ounce fresh lime juice
- 2 strawberries muddled

Instructions:

1. Shake together ingredients and strain over crushed ice.

Tortuga Rum Blend

This delicious creamy rum blend combines El Dorado rum, cinnamon and lemon juice. Garnish with a piece of candied ginger on a skewer.

Servings: 2

Prep Time: 5 minutes

Ingredients:

- 4 ounces El Dorado rum
- 1 ounce simple syrup
- 1 teaspoon orange juice
- ½ teaspoon lemon juice
- ¼ teaspoon cinnamon powder

Instructions:

1. Shake ingredients with ice and strain over fresh ice in glass.

Rum Babalu

Ginger beer, maple syrup, lime juice and Kirk and Sweeney rum come together beautifully to make this delicious drink. Garnish with orange peel.

Servings: 2

Prep Time: 5 minutes

Ingredients:

- 2 ounces Kirk and Sweeney 12 year rum
- 0.5 ounces lime juice
- 1 ounce honey
- 2 ounces ginger beer
- ¼ teaspoon orange zest

Instructions:

1. Shake all ingredients over ice except ginger beer.

2. Strain over fresh ice and pour in ginger beer. Garnish with orange peel.

Rum Fruit Punch

This drink combines different rum flavours, fruit and flower flavours! It's one of my favourites and is perfect for any occasion.

Servings: 2

Prep Time: 5 minutes

Ingredients:

- 2 ounces Bacardi white rum
- 1 ounce El Maestro Sierra Pedro Ximenez Sherry
- 2 ounce Appleton Special Gold rum
- 1 ounce passion fruit puree
- 1 ounce hibiscus syrup
- 1 ounce lemon juice

Instructions:

1. Shake all the ingredients vigorously with ice and strain into a glass.

Pina Colada

This pina colada has a little twist to it. It combines pineapple infused rum, lime juice and Coco Lopez

Servings: 2

Prep Time: 5 minutes

Ingredients:

- 3 ounces pineapple flavoured rum
- 2 ounces pineapple juice
- 0.5 ounce lime juice
- 2 ounces Coco lopez
- 0.75 ounces St. Germain
- Nutmeg for garnish

Instructions:

1. Shake ingredients together and strain over a glass with fresh ice.

2. Garnish with freshly grated nutmeg.

Strawberry Pineapple Cocktail

This simple cocktail comes together with just a few fruity flavours and delicious Bacardi rum.

Servings: 1

Prep Time: 5 minutes

Ingredients:

- 1 ounces Bacardi Superior rum
- 1.5 ounces Pineapple rum
- 0.75 ounce lime juice
- 0.5 simple syrup
- 1 muddled strawberry

Instructions:

1. Shake with ice and strain twice.

Monkey Business

Shake and serve this delicious banana liqueur and rum drink in no time! Garnish with a lime wheel.

Servings: 1

Prep Time: 5 minutes

Ingredients:

- 2 ounces white rum
- 1 ounce Banana liqueur
- 0.5 ounce lime juice
- 0.5 ounce simple syrup

Instructions:

1. Shake over ice and pour into glass.

2. Garnish with lime wheel.

Blue Rum

This drink tastes just as good as it looks! Blue curacao, pineapple juice, coconut rum and lime juice makes this super refreshing.

Servings: 2

Prep Time: 5 minutes

Ingredients:

- 2 ounces spiced rum
- 1 ounce coconut rum
- 3 ounces pineapple juice
- 1 ounce blue curacao
- 1 ounce fresh lime juice

Instructions:

1. Shake ingredients in a shaker with ice and pour into a glass.

Goldeneye Pineapple

Just three ingredients and you'll be able to enjoy this delicious pineapple dark rum drink.

Servings: 1

Prep Time: 5 minutes

Ingredients:

- 1 ounce Blackwell Jamaican rum
- 2 ounces fresh pineapple juice
- 0.75 ounce fresh lime juice

Instructions:

1. Shake with ice, strain and pour over fresh ice.

Wild Cherry

This cocktail is deliciously tart with a little sweetness. Garnish with pineapple and cherries.

Servings: 2

Prep Time: 5 minutes

Ingredients:

- 2 ounces white rum
- 1 ounce lime juice
- 1 ounce pineapple juice
- 1 ounce grapefruit juice
- 2 ounces cherry juice
- 0.75 amarena cherry

Instructions:

1. Shake ingredients in a shaker with ice and pour into a glass.

Caribbean Queen

After a few glasses of this, you'll definitely be feeling like a Caribbean queen! Garnish with fresh pineapples and cherries.

Servings: 2

Prep Time: 5 minutes

Ingredients:

- 3 ounces Mount Gay Black Barrel rum
- 2 ounce pineapple juice
- 1 ounce coconut water
- 0.5 ounce lime juice
- 0.5 ounce lemongrass juice

Instructions:

1. Shake with ice until cold.

2. Strain over a glass of fresh ice.

Boozy Gelato

Pour this over a cold scoop of gelato or vanilla ice cream and you'll have a delicious boozy dessert waiting for you.

Servings: 2

Prep Time: 5 minutes

Ingredients:

- 1 ounce Appleton rum
- 1 ounce Licor 43
- 1 ounce agave nectar
- 4 ounces cold brew coffee

Instructions:

1. Stir together and pour over 2 scoops of gelato.

Pineapple Ginger Cocktail

This is a classic Caribbean pairing, sweet pineapple, spicy ginger and tart lime juice. Garnish with candied ginger and lime wheels.

Servings: 2

Prep Time: 5 minutes

Ingredients:

- 2 ounces El Dorado rum
- 1 ounce ginger syrup
- 1 ounce pineapple juice
- 1 ounce lime juice
- 4 dashes of Angostura Bitters
- 4 ounces club soda

Instructions:

1. Shake with ice and strain into a glass.

2. Top with club soda.

Old Fashioned Bacardi

If it ain't broke don't fix it? This classic drink mixes Bacardi rum with a little sugar and bitters. Garnish with an orange peel.

Servings: 2

Prep Time: 5 minutes

Ingredients:

- 4 ounces Bacardi rum
- 2 teaspoons sugar
- 1 ounce water
- 4 dashes of Angostura Aromatic Bitters

Instructions:

1. Pour ingredients into an old fashioned glass and stir.

2. Add large ice cubes and garnish with orange peel.

Mai Tai

This signature drink will definitely remind you of the Caribbean. Crisp, unique and super delicious.

Servings: 2

Prep Time: 5 minutes

Ingredients:

- 4 ounces Ron Zacapa rum
- 2 ounces lime juice
- 0.5 ounce walnut syrup
- 0.5 ounce lime juice
- 1 ounce Cointreau

Instructions:

1. Shake ingredients over ice and serve on fresh crushed ice.

The Huntmans

This delicious drink is made with dark rum, vodka, simple syrup and lime juice.

Servings: 2

Prep Time: 5 minutes

Ingredients:

- 3 ounces dark rum
- 0.5 ounce vodka
- 1 ounce fresh lime juice
- 1 ounce simple syrup

Instructions:

1. Shake ingredients over ice, strain and serve on fresh crushed ice.

Island Mule

This is a twist on the classic Moscow Mule, it's made with delicious Blackwell rum, ginger beer, lime juice and simple syrup. Garnish with lime wedges.

Servings: 2

Prep Time: 5 minutes

Ingredients:

- 3 ounces dark rum
- 1 ounce white rum
- 1 ounce fresh lime juice
- 1 ounce simple syrup
- 4 ounces ginger beer

Instructions:

1. Shake ingredients except ginger beer over ice.

2. Pour mixture into glass and top with ginger beer.

Conclusion

There we have it, you're now a rum master! You don't need a plane ticket to the Caribbean to enjoy these amazing rum drinks. Indulge in all the delicious flavours of the Caribbean without the sun or messy sand.

You can use whatever dark or white rum you have on hand if you don't have the ones used in these recipes on hand.

About the Author

Heston Brown is an accomplished chef and successful e-book author from Palo Alto California. After studying cooking at The New England Culinary Institute, Heston stopped briefly in Chicago where he was offered head chef at some of the city's most prestigious restaurants. Brown decide that he missed the rolling hills and sunny weather of California and moved back to his home state to open up his own catering company and give private cooking classes.

Heston lives in California with his beautiful wife of 18 years and his two daughters who also have aspirations to follow in their father's footsteps and pursue careers in the culinary arts. Brown is well known for his delicious fish and chicken dishes and teaches these recipes as well as many others to his students.

When Heston gave up his successful chef position in Chicago and moved back to California, a friend suggested he use the internet to share his recipes with the world and so he did! To date, Heston Brown has written over 1000 e-books that contain recipes, cooking tips, business strategies for catering companies and a self-help book he wrote from personal experience.

He claims his wife has been his inspiration throughout many of his endeavours and continues to be his partner in business as well as life. His greatest joy is having all three women in his life in the kitchen with him cooking their favourite meal while his favourite jazz music plays in the background.

Author's Afterthoughts

Thank you to all the readers who invested time and money into my book! I cherish every one of you and hope you took the same pleasure in reading it as I did in writing it.

Out of all of the books out there, you chose mine and for that I am truly grateful. It makes the effort worth it when I know my readers are enjoying my work from beginning to end.

Please take a few minutes to write an Amazon review so that others can benefit from your opinions and insight. Your review will help countless other readers make an informed choice

Thank you so much,

Heston Brown

CPSIA information can be obtained
at www.ICGtesting.com
Printed in the USA
LVHW091408151019
634125LV00035B/2253/P